HOW TO READ
COMPANY FINANCIAL STATEMENTS

How To Read Company Financial Statements

HUGH BECKER
M Comm (Acc)   CA (SA)

Juta & Co, Ltd

CAPE TOWN   WETTON   JOHANNESBURG
1990

First Published 1981
Second Impression 1984
Second Edition 1990
Second Impression 1992
Reprinted 1993

© Juta & Co, Ltd 1992
PO Box 14373, Kenwyn 7790

This book is copyright under the Berne Convention. In terms of the Copyright Act, No 98 of 1978, no part of this book may be reproduced or transmitted in any form or by any means, electronic or mechanical, including photocopying, recording or by any information storage and retrieval system, without permission in writing from the Publisher.

ISBN 0 7021 2352 8

PRINTED AND BOUND IN THE REPUBLIC OF SOUTH AFRICA
BY CREDA PRESS, EPPING

Contents

PREFACE .... (vii)

FINANCIAL STATEMENTS 1
   Auditors' report 1
   Directors' report 1
   Income statement 1
   Balance sheet 9
   Notes to the financial statements 18
   Cash flow statement 18

INTERPRETING THE FINANCIAL STATEMENTS 27
   Liquidity ratios 27
   Leverage ratios 28
   Activity ratios 29
   Profitability 30
   Investment performance 31

Preface

This book makes no pretence at breaking new ground. It has, however, a definite goal: To afford non-experts in the accounting field a basic understanding of financial statements. Investors, managers, businessmen and students with no accounting background should find it especially useful.

A number of people use the information provided by financial reports. As these reports become more informative and complex it becomes increasingly important that users have an understanding of the concepts and figures contained therein.

The meaning and interpretation of concepts and figures are illustrated by means of the financial statements of a fictitious company, Manufacturing Company Limited. Numbering of the items in the financial statements ensures easy cross-reference to the relevant discussion in the text.

Manufacturing Company Limited
Financial Statements
31 December 19.9

Auditors' report

Directors' report

Income statement

Balance sheet

Notes to the financial statements

Cash flow statement

FINANCIAL STATEMENTS

The Companies Act, 1973, requires that financial statements be prepared by companies on an annual basis. Such annual financial statements must at least consist of an auditors' report, a directors' report, an income statement with notes thereto, a balance sheet with notes thereto, and a cash flow statement showing the source and use of all financial resources during the period. When these financial statements are prepared different criteria may be used for the recognition of items to be included in the various sections of the financial statements or for different bases of measurement to be employed. The selection of the criteria or basis of measurement will depend on the social, economic and legal circumstances of the particular company. This fact must be borne in mind when comparing sets of financial statements.

AUDITORS' REPORT

The normal auditors' report highlights the auditors' responsibility and explains the procedures generally applied. It states that the auditors have audited the annual financial statements and that these statements fairly present the financial position of the company at the relevant financial year-end date, the results of the company's operations for the year under review and the cash flow information.

However, before the auditors can issue their report they must comply with extensive requirements laid down by the Companies Act and the Public Accountants' and Auditors' Act. If the auditors are dissatisfied with certain aspects, they will qualify their report accordingly. It is therefore important that the user of financial statements always reads the auditors' report carefully.

DIRECTORS' REPORT

The directors' report deals with all matters which are material to understand the company's—
- nature of business
- profit or loss
- state of affairs

and will, inter alia, contain information on—
- shares and debentures issued during the year
- any major changes in the nature of the company's fixed assets
- dividends paid and/or declared
- the directors and secretary of the company.

This report therefore gives the user of the annual financial statements an overall view of the company and its state of affairs.

INCOME STATEMENT

The income statement shows the results of all the company's operating activities for the financial year under review. It also contains the comparative figures for the preceding year.

An income statement matches revenue received from selling goods or services, against the cost and expenses incurred to achieve those sales. The result is either a net income or a net loss for the year.

Income statements forming part of published financial statements unfortunately only contain limited information, such as turnover, net income before and after tax, and dividends paid/declared. In addition a number of individual items are disclosed by way of notes to the financial statements. The minimum disclosure requirements are set out in Schedule 4 of the Companies Act 1973, as amended. As the income statement contained in this book is to be used for explanatory purposes it contains a few additional items. Many private companies attach a detailed income statement to their annual financial statements. Companies also regularly prepare detailed statements for management purposes. Furthermore, all companies have to include detailed income statements with their financial statements submitted to the Receiver of Revenue. In the detailed income statements items such as directors emoluments (refer item 7 page 3) and depreciation (refer item 6 page 3) are allocated between the administrative and production sectors of the business. For disclosure purposes, in terms of the Companies Act, these items are aggregated.

MANUFACTURING COMPANY LIMITED

INCOME STATEMENT for the year ended 31 December 19.9

		19.9 R'000	19.8 R'000
1	Turnover	38 945	33 024
2	Sales	38 945	33 024
3	Cost of goods sold	30 959	26 071
4	Gross profit	7 986	6 953
	Expenditure	1 694	1 495
5	Selling and administrative expenses	825	737
6	Depreciation	347	302
7	Directors' emoluments	522	456
8	Operating income	6 292	5 458
9	Other income	171	140
	Dividends from unlisted investments	144	140
	Surplus on disposal of fixed assets	27	—
10	Net income before finance charges	6 463	5 598
11	Interest paid	977	686
12	Net income before taxation	5 486	4 912
13	Taxation	2 350	2 253
14	Net income after taxation	3 136	2 659
15	Share of after-tax income of associated company	93	81
16	Net income	3 229	2 740
17	Preference dividends	28	28
18	Net income attributable to ordinary shareholders	3 201	2 712
19	Ordinary dividends	1 008	882
20	Retained income for the year	2 193	1 830
21	Retained income at beginning of year	7 355	5 525
22	Retained income at end of year	9 548	7 355
		Cents	*Cents*
23	Earnings per ordinary share	38,1	32,3

Turnover

This figure represents the aggregate turnover for the year under review, i e all sales (net of discounts to customers and value added tax). It may be disclosed as a percentage increase or decrease on the aggregate turnover for the preceding financial year.

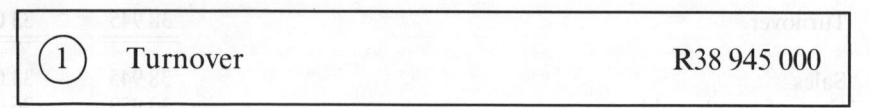

> (1) Turnover   R38 945 000

Sales

This is normally the equivalent of turnover. It represents the income received by the company for its main trading activities, the sale of goods and/or services. This figure is shown after deducting discounts allowed to customers and value added tax.

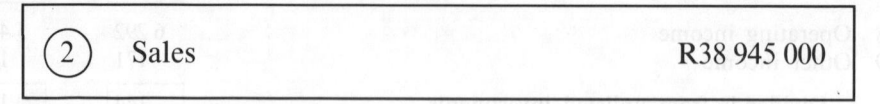

> (2) Sales   R38 945 000

In published financial statements where only the legislated disclosure is stated, items 2, 3, 4 and 5 will not be separately identified.

Cost of goods sold

For companies engaged in manufacture, this figure includes the cost of raw materials, the cost of factory labour, and other factory overheads (electricity, rent, supervision) which are necessary to produce finished goods for sale. Depreciation relating to manufacturing plant and equipment is also regarded as a production cost.

This is usually the largest single cost item in the income statement of a manufacturing company.

> (3) Cost of goods sold   R30 959 000

Gross profit

This is the difference between the total selling price of the goods sold (net of discounts and value added tax) and the cost thereof.

> (4) Gross profit   R7 986 000

Selling and administrative expenses

These expenses include the costs incurred to sell the manufactured product, e g advertising and promotion, salesmen's salaries and commissions, office expenses and distribution or freight costs.

| ⑤ | Selling and administrative expenses | R825 000 |

Depreciation

The cost of most fixed assets (e g plant, equipment, motor vehicles, buildings, but not land) is allocated to the business over the useful life of the individual assets. For this reason, a proportion of the initial cost of the asset is deducted each year from the asset to show its reduced value, which represents an expense to the business known as depreciation which is deducted in the income statement. The portion relating to manufacturing assets is regarded as a production cost and the balance (below) is charged to the appropriate section(s) in the income statement. For disclosure purposes in published financial statements the total depreciation figure for the business is disclosed.

| ⑥ | Depreciation | R347 000 |

Directors' emoluments

This item comprises the total remuneration accrued to all the directors of the company. It includes the salaries of directors who are full-time employees of the company (executive directors) as well as the fees paid to non-executive directors.

| ⑦ | Directors' emoluments | R522 000 |

Operating income

This is the residual figure after deducting cost of goods sold, depreciation and all selling and administrative expenses from sales, i e the net income generated by the company's fundamental operations.

| ⑧ | Operating income | R6 292 000 |

Other income

At this point income from sources other than normal company operations is added.

⑨	Other income	
	Dividends from unlisted investments	R144 000
	Surplus on disposal of fixed assets	27 000

Net income before finance charges

The company's net income before taking into account interest paid to financiers is therefore:

> ⑩   Net income before finance charges   R6 463 000

Interest paid

This item reflects the cost of utilising interest bearing debt. Manufacturing Company Limited has long-term loans of R7m which bear interest at 15% per annum. In addition thereto, the company has short-term borrowings and utilises an overdraft facility at its bank in order to finance short-term capital requirements. The interest payable on short-term financing is normally higher than that payable on long-term debt.

Interest represents a fixed obligation and must be paid regularly regardless of whether a company makes a profit or not.

> ⑪   Interest paid   R977 000

Net income before taxation

The deduction of interest paid from item 10 results in:

> ⑫   Net income before taxation   R5 486 000

Taxation

The *effective* tax rate in this example is 42,8%, although the normal corporate tax rate for 1991 is 48%. This occurs whenever the allowances granted for tax purposes exceed those provided for in the accounting records or the company has non-taxable income. The notes to the financial statements will contain a reconciliation of the effective rate with the normal rate, stating and quantifying the reasons for the variance. A common explanation is the timing of the tax allowances granted on capital equipment purchased.

> ⑬   Taxation   R2 350 000

Net income after taxation

This amount is derived after adding other income to sales, and deducting all expenses and costs, including tax.

| ⑭ | Net income after taxation | R3 136 000 |

Share of after-tax income of associated company

An associated company is one in which an investing company exercises significant influence.

A proportion of the associated company's after-tax income, apportioned on the basis of the number of shares held in the associate, accrues to Manufacturing Company Limited: Significant influence is presumed where an investor holds 20% or more of the voting power of the investee unless demonstrated to the contrary. Where an investing company is a member of and exercises control over another company the investee becomes known as a subsidiary company. Once a company has subsidiaries and associates the company then produces group financial statements in addition to its own financial statements, The most common form of group financial statements is that of consolidated financial statements which are beyond the scope of this book.

| ⑮ | Share of after-tax income of associated company | R93 000 |

Net income

The final net income for the year, i e total income less all costs, expenses and tax, is arrived at:

| ⑯ | Net income | R3 229 000 |

Preference dividends

Preference shares are normally shares without voting rights issued by a company and which carry a fixed dividend (in this example 10%).

When preference shares are *cumulative*, it means that in years where a net loss after tax is made and preference dividends are not paid, arrear dividends *accumulate* until the company makes profits again. The arrear dividends on preference shares are then paid before *ordinary* shareholders receive further dividends. In this example it is assumed that the preference dividends are up to date. The total due is 10% × R280 000 (refer item 27 page 10).

| ⑰ | Preference dividends | R28 000 |

Note that preference dividends are deducted *after* tax is accounted for. This is so because the Receiver of Revenue regards preference dividends in the same light as *ordinary* dividends and they are, therefore, not deductible as an expense (as interest is) before tax is calculated.

Net income attributable to ordinary shareholders
Once preference dividends have been deducted, what is left of net income belongs to the ordinary shareholders.

| (18) | Net income attributable to ordinary shareholders | R3 201 000 |

This amount may either be wholly retained in the company as part of the reserves, or some of it may be distributed to the ordinary shareholders as dividends.

| (19) | Ordinary dividends | R1 008 000 |

Thus a total dividend of 12 cents per share (8,4m ordinary shares in issue) accrued to the ordinary shareholders in respect of the year under review.

Retained income
Reserves are built up for a variety of reasons, i e to provide —
- a 'cushion' for bad trading years
- for the replacement of plant, vehicles and equipment
- for the continuous higher investment in stock and other working capital items necessitated by inflation
- for the expansion of the business.

The reserves from previous years are added to the reserves from the current year, and a new retained income figure is obtained.

(20)	Retained income for the year	R2 193 000
(21)	Retained income at beginning of year	R7 355 000
(22)	Retained income at end of year	R9 548 000

Earnings per share
This is the net amount of income for the year (in cents) attributable to each ordinary share. It is calculated by dividing the earnings attributable to equity

(ordinary) shareholders (R3 201 000 refer item 18 page 3) by the number of ordinary shares in issue (8,4 million).

> (23) Earnings per ordinary share   38,1c

BALANCE SHEET

Whilst the income statement reflects a record of all the ongoing transactions and activities for the financial year (cf a motion picture), the balance sheet is drawn up for a specific moment in time — in essence, a 'snapshot' of the company's assets and liabilities at a certain point in time.

The asset and liability items of the balance sheet always balance. This is because the liabilities show who has provided the company's funds, while the assets show how these funds have been used (or employed) in the business.

The typical structure of a balance sheet appears overleaf. It shows two principal categories — *capital employed* (consisting of shareholders' funds on the one hand and long-term debts to outsiders on the other hand) and *employment of capital* (the assets). The net current situation reflecting current assets less current liabilities is disclosed under the employment of capital category.

MANUFACTURING COMPANY LIMITED

BALANCE SHEET at 31 December 19.9

		19.9 R'000	19.8 R'000
	CAPITAL EMPLOYED		
24	Ordinary share capital		
	Authorised		
	10 000 000 ordinary shares of R1 each	10 000	10 000
	Issued		
	8 400 000 ordinary shares of R1 each	8 400	8 400
25	Distributable reserve	9 548	7 355
	Retained income		
26	Ordinary shareholders' interest	17 948	15 755
27	Preference share capital		
	Authorised and issued	280	280
	140 000 10% cumulative preference shares of R2 each		
28	Share capital and reserves	18 228	16 035
29	Long-term liabilities	7 000	4 000
	Long-term loans (interest 15% p a)		
30	Total capital employed	25 228	20 035
	EMPLOYMENT OF CAPITAL		
31	Fixed assets	6 808	4 138
32	At cost	9 922	7 004
33	*Less* Accumulated depreciation	3 114	2 866
	Investments—unlisted	2 412	2 275
34	Associated company	878	785
35	Other companies	1 534	1 490
36	Net current assets	16 008	13 622
37	*Current assets*		
38	Stock	12 148	9 276
39	Accounts receivable (Debtors)	10 231	8 430
40	Taxation	—	17
41	Cash at bank	—	32
		22 379	17 755
42	*Less Current liabilities*		
43	Accounts payable (Creditors)	5 270	3 629
44	Short-term borrowings	300	—
45	Taxation	95	—
46	Shareholders for dividend	588	504
47	Bank overdraft	118	—
		6 371	4 133
48	Total employment of capital	25 228	20 035

Capital employed

The first part of the balance sheet consists of the long-term sources of financing utilised by the company. The providers of capital can be classified as shareholders and outsiders.

Ordinary share capital

Two subheadings appear under this item (or, normally in a note to the financial statements), i e the nominal capital—number of shares and nominal value of each share—that the company is *authorised* to issue, and secondly, the nominal capital that has actually been *issued* to the ordinary shareholders (owners) of the company.

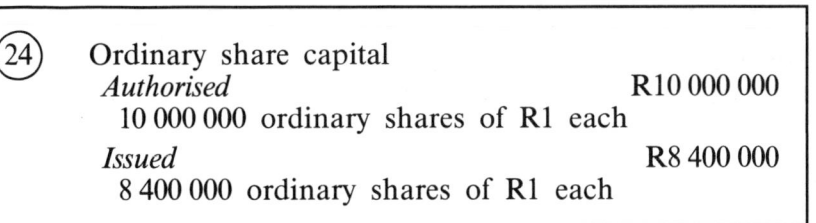

> (24) Ordinary share capital
> *Authorised* R10 000 000
> 10 000 000 ordinary shares of R1 each
> *Issued* R8 400 000
> 8 400 000 ordinary shares of R1 each

Ordinary share capital may not normally be returned to the shareholders unless the company is wound up. In this example the R1 reflects the 'par' value of the share. Companies may choose to have shares of 'no par' value.

Distributable reserve

When a company starts business it normally only has the share capital provided by its shareholders. However, the major portion of annual after-tax earnings is usually retained and accumulated to provide further capital for various reasons (see discussion of items 20–22). The retained income figure thus represents the total cumulative after-tax earnings of the company since its inception, less all distributions to shareholders by way of dividends.

By the end of 19.9 this figure has grown to

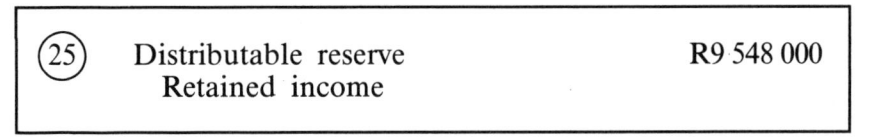

> (25) Distributable reserve R9 548 000
> Retained income

Technically this amount may be distributed to the ordinary shareholders, i e the owners of the company, in the form of dividends. Doing this could, however, create a major liquidity problem for the company.

A company can also have *non-distributable reserves*. These reserves may arise in the first instance because the price at which the shares are issued is *greater* than the nominal value of the share. Any excess of issue price over nominal value is known as the share premium. The premium is classified as a non-distributable reserve. Also, other transfers from the income statement may be made to this reserve by the company from time to time e.g. when assets are revalued to reflect their market value as opposed to historic cost.

One important difference between non-distributable reserves and distributable reserves is that the former cannot be distributed to shareholders until the company is finally wound up.

Owners' equity

The total ordinary shareholders' funds (due to the ordinary shareholders if the business were dissolved on the balance sheet date) is the sum of ordinary share capital, non-distributable reserves and distributable reserves.

> (26) Ordinary shareholders' interest   R17 948 000

This amount would be realised, however, only if the assets of the business could be sold at the amounts shown in the balance sheet. In general, the break-up value of a company is somewhat less than the book values shown in the balance sheet.

Preference share capital

The rights attached to preference shares have already been discussed as part of the analysis of the income statement.

Preference shares are issued, like ordinary shares, for a specific value, for example:

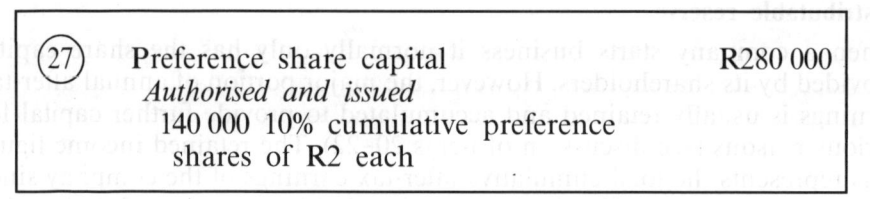

> (27) Preference share capital   R280 000
> *Authorised and issued*
> 140 000 10% cumulative preference shares of R2 each

Although the preference shareholders are not co-owners of the company, the preference shares form part of the company's total share capital and are not treated as borrowed funds.

Ordinary shareholders' interest and preference share capital are added to produce:

> (28) Share capital and reserves   R18 228 000

Long-term liabilities

Debts owed by the company which are due more than one year from the date of the balance sheet are regarded as long-term liabilities.

In the case of Manufacturing Company Limited, the only long-term liabilities are loans which must be fully repaid in, say, 10 equal annual instalments.

Usually long-term debt is 'secured' by the pledge or cession of specific fixed assets for the duration of the loan. If the company defaults by not paying either the annual interest or the equal annual repayments of the initial sum borrowed, the secured assets may be sold and the proceeds used to repay the debt plus unpaid interest.

'Unsecured' means that the debt is not secured over specific assets, and in the case of default or of bankruptcy, the creditor's claim against the company ranks with other creditors' claims.

> (29) Long-term liabilities   R7 000 000
> Long-term loans

Total capital employed

The total of all the long-term sources of capital and debt are added to produce

> (30) Total capital employed   R25 228 000

Employment of capital

The balance sheet items listed under this heading generally refer to the assets in which the long-term funds in the business (the capital employed) have been invested to support business activities.

Fixed assets

This item usually refers to property (land and buildings), plant, equipment and machinery, furniture, fixtures and motor vehicles. These assets are not acquired for resale, but are used for the manufacture, warehousing and transportation of goods.

Fixed assets are usually shown in the balance sheet at a *net* amount, i e intitial cost *less* total depreciation to date. There is, however, a tendency towards regular revaluation of fixed assets, in which instance the relevant asset(s) will be shown at valuation less total depreciation since date of valuation.

The different categories of fixed assets, initial cost/valuation and accumulated depreciation will be disclosed by way of a note to the financial statements.

Depreciation

Charging a proportion of the cost of fixed assets against income in the income statement each year serves the purpose of *allocating the cost* of an asset over its useful life.

Fixed assets normally decline in value owing to wear and tear, obsolescence, new technology or the passage of time. For example, Manufacturing

Company Limited purchases a new machine costing R36 000. It has a life of 8 years and straight-line depreciation will be charged (i e one-eighth of the cost of the machine will be deducted each year for 8 years, after which it will have a book value of zero).

The balance sheet at the end of the first and second year would show:

```
Year 1
Machine (at cost)..........................         R36 000
Less Accumulated depreciation (36 000/8) ...          4 500
Net depreciated value.......................        R31 500

Year 2
Machine (at cost)..........................         R36 000
Less Accumulated depreciation..............           9 000
Net depreciated value.......................        R27 000
```

In the current balance sheet, the net fixed asset figure is derived as follows:

㉛	Fixed assets	R6 808 000
㉜	At cost	9 922 000
㉝	Less Accumulated depreciation	3 114 000

Investments

Companies have to disclose their aggregate investments in listed and unlisted securities separately from one another. Furthermore, investments in associated companies (already discussed as part of the analysis of the income statement) have to be disclosed separately from other investments. Associated companies are shown at carrying value, i e the original cost of the investment *plus* all after-tax income accrued to the investment and not distributed by way of dividends.

In the case of Manufacturing Company Limited's investment in its associated company the carrying value was R785 000 at the end of the previous financial year (19.8). The company's share of the after-tax income of its associated company is R93 000 in respect of 19.9 (see item 15 in the income statement). No dividends have been received from this investment, therefore the total amount accrues and is added to the previous carrying value, resulting in a current carrying value of R878 000.

	Investments — *unlisted*	R2 412 000
(34)	Associated company	878 000
(35)	Other companies	1 534 000

The market value of listed investments and the directors' valuation of unlisted investments will be disclosed in a note to the financial statements.

Net current assets

The total of all current liabilities is subtracted from the total current assets figure to derive net current assets (also known as net working capital).

This essentially shows the amount of current assets which are permanently funded from long-term (capital employed), rather than short-term sources (i e the current liabilities).

(36)	Net current assets	R16 008 000
(37)	Current assets	22 379 000
(42)	*Less* Current liabilities	6 371 000

Current assets

Generally, current assets include cash and those assets which will be converted into cash within one year.

The company's total current assets amount to

(37)	Current assets	R22 379 000

Stock

This item is composed of raw materials, consumables, work in progress, and completed manufactured products.

Raw materials are usually valued at cost, or at their current realisable value if this amount is lower.

Work in progress is valued at the lower of the cost of raw materials, direct labour and a proportion of production overhead expense or the net realisable value of those items.

Manufactured products (finished goods) are valued at raw material cost plus direct labour cost plus production overhead expenses, or at current realisable value, whichever is lower.

> (38) Stock   R12 148 000

Accounts receivable (Debtors)

This amount shows the value of credit sales to customers not yet collected in cash. Usual credit terms may be 30, 60 or 90 days.

> (39) Accounts receivable (Debtors)   R10 231 000

Prepaid taxation

Companies are required to estimate their annual pre-tax income and pay provisional tax on this estimate. Frequently, companies may over-estimate, thus paying too much provisional tax, like Manufacturing Company Limited did in 19.8. The amount due by the Receiver of Revenue is shown under current assets (comparative figure):

> (40) Taxation   R17 000

Cash at bank

This is the amount of cash held by the company's bankers at the financial year-end and is the company's most liquid asset.

The company had no cash at its bank at the end of 19.9, but the position in the previous year (i.e *31 December 19.8*) was:

> (41) Cash at bank   R32 000

Current liabilities

This category includes all short-term debts of the company which will become due within a year of the balance sheet date. The time parameter corresponds with that applied in the definition of current assets.

Total current liabilities amount to

> (42) Current liabilities   R6 371 000

Accounts payable (Creditors)

This item represents the amounts that the company owes to all creditors who have supplied goods or services necessary for the company's ongoing trading and other business operations.

> ㊸ Accounts payable (Creditors)　　　　R5 270 000

Short-term borrowings
This item mainly refers to loans which fall due within a year of the balance sheet date. It normally includes the current portion due in respect of long-term borrowings.

> ㊹ Short-term borrowings　　　　R300 000

Taxation payable
This figure represents an *accrued expense*, i e income tax due to the Receiver of Revenue but not yet paid at balance sheet date.

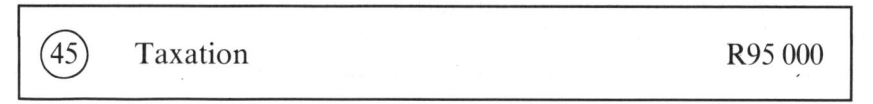

> ㊺ Taxation　　　　R95 000

Other items of accrued expenditure frequently occur in balance sheets and are normally included with accounts payable. Common examples are leave pay due to employees and ongoing monthly expenditure in respect of electricity, telephone and operating leases.

Shareholders for dividend
This item indicates that part of the total dividend declared (as per the income statement) which has not yet been paid in full at the balance sheet date. Companies often pay dividends twice a year—an interim dividend during the year, and a final dividend, declared in respect of the year but only paid after year-end.

The unpaid portion of the dividend at the balance sheet date is therefore

> ㊻ Shareholders for dividend　　　　R588 000

Bank overdraft
During peak seasons of manufacturing and selling, it is usually necessary for a business to request an overdraft from its bank for 'bridging finance'. The company's employees need to be paid for their labour and services, and suppliers require payment for materials. Until credit customers (accounts receivable) settle their accounts due to the business, there is little cash coming in, while large sums—for payment of labour and suppliers—are going out. The gap (or shortfall) between the two is met through a bank overdraft.

> (47) Bank overdraft   R118 000

Total employment of capital
Finally, the total of all the company's assets (fixed assets, investments and net current assets) funded by the total long-term capital employed in the company, amount to

> (48) Total employment of capital   R25 228 000

NOTES TO THE FINANCIAL STATEMENTS

Not all the useful information is provided in the income statement and balance sheet. A lot more detail and clarification are available in the notes to the financial statements. It is therefore very important to read the items in the financial statements in conjunction with the relevant (cross-referenced) notes.

The notes also provide a statement of the accounting policies adopted by the company, and a detailed break-down of assets and liabilities.

Items to be watched closely are *contingent liabilities* and *future capital expenditure.*

Contingent liabilities indicate amounts which the company *may* be called upon to pay in the future, e g legal disputes.

Future capital expenditure indicates the amounts the company intends to spend on the replacement of existing facilities and new plant expansion. A manufacturing company which does *not* undertake new capital expenditure is impairing its future growth and competitive position. This aspect will, inter alia, also be evident from the cash flow statement.

CASH FLOW STATEMENT

The cash flow statement provides useful information on the sources of funds generated and raised, and how these funds were utilised by the company. Cash flow statements which appear in published financial statements usually have a logical format. It begins with the cash generated by the company's operations, from which cash is utilised to pay interest and taxation, and to make distributions to shareholders (in this sequence). Next it deals with the cash invested during the year to maintain and expand operations. Finally, it states the external sources of cash utilised to finance the effects of the aforementioned cash flows.

MANUFACTURING COMPANY LIMITED

CASH FLOW STATEMENT for the year ended 31 December 19.9

		Note	19.9 *R'000*
49	**Cash retained from operating activities**		84
50	Cash generated by operations	1	7 139
51	Investment income		144
52	Utilised to increase working capital	2	(3 032)
53	Cash generated by operating activities		4 251
54	Finance costs		(977)
55	Taxation paid	3	(2 238)
56	Cash available from operating activities		1 036
57	Dividends paid	4	(952)
58	**Cash utilised in investing activities**		(3 534)
59	Investment to maintain operations:		
	Replacement of fixed assets	5	(926)
	Proceeds on disposal of fixed assets		110
			(816)
60	Investment to expand operations:		
	Additions to fixed assets	6	(2 674)
	Purchase of shares in unlisted company		(44)
			(2 718)
61	**Cash utilised**		(3 450)
62	**Cash effects of financing activities:**		
63	Increase in long-term borrowings		3 000
64	Increase in short-term borrowings		418
65	Decrease in cash at bank		32
			3 450

(NB: Formal cash flow statements will provide comparative figures.)

NOTES TO THE CASH FLOW STATEMENT

	19.9 R'000
1 Cash generated by operations:	
Operating income before interest and taxation	6 463
Adjustment for:	
Depreciation	847
Profit on disposal of fixed assets	(27)
Investment income	(144)
	7 139
2 Cash utilised to increase working capital:	
Increase in stocks	2 872
Increase in debtors	1 801
Increase in creditors	(1 641)
	3 032
3 Taxation paid is reconciled to the amounts disclosed in the income statement as follows:	
Amount prepaid at beginning of year	(17)
Amount charged to income statement	2 350
Amount unpaid at end of year	(95)
Cash amounts paid	2 238
4 Dividends paid is reconciled to the amount disclosed in the income statement as follows:	
Amount unpaid at beginning of year	504
Amount charged to income statement	1 036
Amount unpaid at end of year	(588)
Cash amounts paid	952
5 Replacement of fixed assets:	
Plant and machinery	714
Vehicles	212
	926
6 Additions to fixed assets:	
Land and buildings	1 700
Plant and machinery	644
Vehicles	137
Office equipment	193
	2 674

Cash generated by operations

The primary source of a company's funds during the year is the net amount left after subtracting all operating expenses from the annual income.

However, to arrive at a figure for cash generated by the company's business operations, the net income figure must be adjusted (see note 1 to the cash flow statement).

Firstly, *annual depreciation*, although it is shown as an *expense* in the income statement, does *not* require an outlay of cash. As the cash flow statement is concerned with *actual* movements of funds during the year, it is necessary to *add back* the depreciation expense to show the true picture for the flow of funds. (Assume that cost of sales includes R500 000 depreciation on production plant and machinery, bringing depreciation for the year to R847 000.)

Included in net income is also an amount for the profit or surplus earned by the company upon selling some of its fixed assets. Since the total cash proceeds on the disposal of fixed assets is stated separately (see item 59), this surplus should be excluded from the company's normal profits from operations.

Finally, one further adjustment must be made before the actual figure for cash generated by operations emerges, viz investment income, which does not form part of the company's primary business operations and will be separately disclosed.

The net result (as calculated in note 1 to the cash flow statement) is

(50)	Cash generated by operations	R7 139 000

Cash generated by operating activities

In order to arrive at the net cash generated by all the company's activities, income from investments is added, and the funds utilised to increase working capital are deducted from cash generated by operations. Note that the increases in the company's stock and debtors during the year are partly funded by an increase in creditors (accounts payable) (see note 2 to the cash flow statement).

(50)	Cash generated by operations	R7 139 000
(51)	Investment income	144 000
(52)	Utilised to increase working capital	(3 032 000)
(53)	Cash generated by operating activities	R4 251 000

Cash available from operating activities

This is determined after providing for the cash amounts paid to external providers of finance (interest) and the Receiver of Revenue (income tax) during the year.

(53)	Cash generated by operating activities	R4 251 000
(54)	Finance costs	(977 000)
(55)	Taxation paid	(2 238 000)
(56)	Cash available from operating activities	R1 036 000

Cash retained from operating activities

Next the cash distributed to the shareholders (the providers of permanent capital) is deducted in order to arrive at the internally generated cash which was retained by the company.

(56)	Cash available from operating activities	R1 036 000
(57)	Dividends paid	(952 000)
(49)	Cash retained from operating activities	R 84 000

It is important to note that although Manufacturing Company Limited's income statement shows a *retained income* of R2 193 000 for the year (item 20), the company in fact had *retained cash* of only R84 000.

Cash utilised in investing activities

A distinction is drawn between the cash invested to maintain activities and that invested to expand operations. The latter indicates the extent to which the company applied funds to ensure future growth.

(59)	Investment to maintain operations	R 816 000
(60)	Investment to expand operations	(2 718 000)
(58)	Cash utilised in investing activities	R3 534 000

Total cash utilised

The net cash effect of all the above cash flows, positive and negative, is

| ㉖ | Cash utilised | R3 450 000 |

Financing activities

The final part of the cash flow statement discloses how the net cash outflow of the company (item 61) was financed:

㉓	Increase in long-term borrowings	R3 000 000
㉔	Increase in short-term borrowings	418 000
㉕	Decrease in cash at bank	32 000
㉒	Cash effects of financing activities	R3 450 000

Interpreting the Financial Statements

Liquidity ratios

Leverage ratios

Activity ratios

Profitability

Investment performance

INTERPRETING THE FINANCIAL STATEMENTS

In order to evaluate the company's financial results and state of affairs, the information presented in the financial statements has to be converted/processed further so that some meaningful interpretation can be derived showing how the business is performing in terms of

    (a) its own past performance and financial position
    (b) other companies in the same industry.

This can be obtained by expressing key figures in the financial statements as *ratios* and *percentages*.

These can be classified for convenience into five major categories:
    LIQUIDITY RATIOS
    LEVERAGE (OR GEARING) RATIOS
    ACTIVITY RATIOS
    PROFITABILITY RATIOS
    INVESTMENT PERFORMANCE RATIOS.

LIQUIDITY RATIOS

These ratios measure the ability of the company to pay its current liabilities out of current assets.

Current ratio

The most commonly used ratio is the current ratio, which is calculated by dividing current assets by current liabilities:

(37) $\dfrac{\text{Current assets}}{\text{Current liabilities}} = \dfrac{\text{R22 379 000}}{\text{R 6 371 000}} = 3{,}5 : 1$
(42)

Each R1 of current liabilities is covered by R3,5 of current assets. Banks and other short-term lenders of money look for a ratio of 2 : 1 in an average manufacturing concern, so Manufacturing Company Limited is in an extremely healthy position.

Quick ratio or acid test

As stocks are the *least* liquid of all current assets, a more conservative test of the ability of the company to meet its short-term maturing obligations is to subtract the stock figure from current assets and then divide the balance (i e the more liquid assets) by current liabilities.

(37) Current assets   R22 379 000
(38) *Less* Stock   12 148 000
     'Quick assets'   R10 231 000

$\dfrac{\text{Quick assets}}{\text{Current liabilities}} = \dfrac{\text{R10 231 000}}{\text{R 6 371 000}} = 1{,}6 : 1$

This is still a healthy figure. Most lenders expect a quick ratio of between 1 and 1,5.

LEVERAGE RATIOS

These ratios provide a measure of the extent to which borrowed funds are used to finance company assets.

The *greater* the proportion of borrowed funds, the greater the financial risk to the lenders. This, in turn, pushes up the interest rate on new borrowings as the additional risk is taken into account.

Total debt/Total assets

This ratio is calculated by adding the *total* liabilities of the business and dividing by total assets.

(29)	Long-term liabilities	R 7 000 000
(42)	Current liabilities	6 371 000
	Total debt	R13 371 000
(31)	Fixed assets	R 6 808 000
	Investments	2 412 000
(37)	Current assets	22 379 000
	Total assets	R31 599 000

$$\frac{\text{Total debt}}{\text{Total assets}} = \frac{\text{R13 371 000}}{\text{R31 599 000}} \times 100\% = 42,3\%$$

The ratio is fairly good. Where a company has *more than* 50% of its assets funded by debt the creditors, rather than the shareholders, are supplying most of the finances and therefore bear most of the risk.

Long-term debt/Capital employed (Debt : equity ratio)

The total debt ratio shown above includes short-term borrowings. The providers of long-term debt are more interested in knowing how much of the *long-term* capital is provided by debt:

$$\frac{\text{(29) Long-term liabilities}}{\text{(30) Total capital employed}} = \frac{\text{R 7 000 000}}{\text{R25 228 000}} \times 100\% = 27,7\%$$

Although circumstances will vary from industry to industry, percentages below 50% are usually considered acceptable. The *age* of the company is a key factor here, as new companies in growing industries should be funded as far as possible from equity (shareholders' funds).

Interest cover

This measure indicates the extent to which interest on debt can be met by company earnings. A business which cannot earn sufficient to cover its interest payments is unprofitable.

$$\frac{(10) \text{ Total income}}{(11) \text{ Interest paid}} = \frac{R\ 6\ 463\ 000}{R\ \ \ 977\ 000} = 6{,}6 \text{ times}$$

An interest cover of 3 times is generally expected by lenders.

ACTIVITY RATIOS

These are measures of business efficiency in the management of two key current assets, namely stock and accounts receivable (debtors), and the settlement of accounts payable (creditors).

Stock turnover

A business carrying too much stock ties up capital and runs the risk of product obsolescence and stock deterioration. Stock turnover is measured as cost of goods sold divided by stock.

$$\frac{(3) \text{ Cost of goods sold}}{(38) \text{ Stock}} = \frac{R30\ 959\ 000}{R12\ 148\ 000} = 2{,}5 \text{ times a year.}$$

This means that the value of inventory on hand at the balance sheet date will take about 5 months to sell completely (12 months/2,5). This may be satisfactory for sectors of the clothing industry, but would be disastrous for a supermarket chain.

Accounts receivable (debtors) collection period

The credit terms granted to customers are partly determined by generally accepted trade practice, and partly by the efficiency of the company's credit control department.

Slow-paying customers tie up working capital and force the company to seek bridging finance for longer periods.

The collection period is calculated by

(a) determining daily credit sales; then
(b) dividing daily credit sales into the accounts receivable balance. This will indicate how many days it takes for daily credit sales to be collected. (Assume that credit sales amounted to R30m.)

(a) Daily credit sales $= \dfrac{\text{Credit sales}}{365 \text{ days}} = \dfrac{R30\ 000\ 000}{365 \text{ days}}$

$= R82\ 192$ per day.

Where necessary the 365 is replaced by the number of actual trading days in the current year.

(b) Collection period = ㊳ $\dfrac{\text{Accounts receivable}}{\text{Daily credit sales}}$ = $\dfrac{\text{R10 231 000}}{\text{R82 192}}$

= 124 days.

In other words, debtors are taking on average 4 months to pay. This is an unacceptably long time, as the collection period should normally not exceed 90 days.

Accounts payable (creditors) settlement period

Associated with the preceding two ratios is the period for which suppliers' accounts are outstanding. The same principles applicable to the calculation of the debtors collection period are applied. However, whereas accounts receivable relate to credit sales, accounts payable pertain to purchases on credit (assume R25m for the year).

(a) Daily credit purchases = $\dfrac{\text{Total credit purchases}}{365 \text{ days}}$

= $\dfrac{\text{R25 000 000}}{365 \text{ days}}$ = R68 493 per day

(b) Settlement period = $\dfrac{\text{Accounts payable}}{\text{Daily credit purchases}}$

= ㊸ $\dfrac{\text{R5 270 000}}{\text{R68 493}}$

= 77 days.

Although slightly long, it is not exceptional for a manufacturing concern which enjoys a good relationship with its suppliers.

PROFITABILITY

The ability of a company to generate profits is essential to its long-term survival. Profits are necessary to sustain growth, to attract new capital and to reward shareholders for risk-taking.

Gross profit

This indicates the profitability of basic trading and manufacturing operations:

Gross profit margin % =

$$\frac{\text{\textcircled{4} Gross profit}}{\text{\textcircled{2} Sales}} = \frac{R\ 7\ 986\ 000}{R38\ 945\ 000} \times 100\% = 20{,}5\%$$

This means that each rand of sales contains a gross profit of 20,5c. Changes in proft margin from previous years are an important indication of efficiency, types of products manufactured and the intensity of competitive activity. Strong competition will tend to force down prices and therefore lower profit margins.

Net profit margin

This measure indicates the profitability after *all* expenses including tax and preference dividends have been deducted.

Net profit margin % =

$$\frac{\text{\textcircled{18} Net income}}{\text{\textcircled{2} Sales}} = \frac{R\ 3\ 201\ 000}{R38\ 945\ 000} \times 100\% = 8{,}2\%$$

Return on shareholders' funds

The net income attributable to ordinary shareholders is also used to calculate the return on shareholders' funds, which is one of the most important measures of the return to ordinary shareholders.

Return on shareholders' funds =

$$\frac{\text{\textcircled{18} Net income}}{\text{\textcircled{26} Ordinary shareholders' interest}} = \frac{R\ 3\ 201\ 000}{R17\ 948\ 000} \times 100\% = 17{,}8\%$$

INVESTMENT PERFORMANCE

The major limitation to using the preceding measure is that the balance sheet figure for shareholders' interest/funds is usually different from the *current market value* of a listed company's shares. For new or potential investors, this is obviously the most important measure.

There are several performance measures which are traditionally used in the measurement of share performance.

Earnings yield

This is calculated by dividing earnings per share by the current market price of ordinary shares (assume 205c) and indicates the current income producing power per ordinary share at the current market price.

$$\frac{\text{\textcircled{23} Earnings per share}}{\text{Current market price}} = \frac{38{,}1c}{205c} \times 100\% = 18{,}6\%$$

Price/earnings ratio

The P/E ratio indicates the number of years the earnings (at current level) will take to equal the current market price.

It is determined by dividing the market price per share by the earnings per share (thus the reciprocal of earnings yield).

$$\frac{\text{Market price per share}}{\text{Earnings per share}} = \frac{205c}{38,1c}$$

$$\therefore \text{P/E ratio} = 5,4$$

Dividend yield

As the full earnings per share are seldom paid out to shareholders, the dividend paid is a more accurate measure of the ordinary shareholders' return on investment.

Dividend per share:

$$\frac{\text{⑲ Ordinary dividends}}{\text{㉔ }\textit{Number}\text{ of issued ordinary shares}} = \frac{R1\ 008\ 000}{8\ 400\ 000} = 12c \text{ per share}$$

Dividend yield:

$$\frac{\text{Dividend per share}}{\text{Current market price}} = \frac{12c}{205c} \times 100\% = 5,9\%$$

Dividend cover

The dividend cover indicates the number of times that the current earnings attributable to ordinary shareholders exceed the current ordinary dividends.

$$\frac{\text{⑱ Attributable earnings}}{\text{⑲ Ordinary dividends}} = \frac{R3\ 201\ 000}{R1\ 008\ 000} = 3,2 \text{ times}$$

or

$$\frac{\text{㉓ Earnings per share}}{\text{Dividend per share}} = \frac{38,1c}{12c} = 3,2 \text{ times}$$

The reciprocal measures the proportion of current earnings that is distributed as ordinary dividends:

(23) $$\frac{\text{Dividend per share}}{\text{Earnings per share}} = \frac{12c}{38,1c} \times 100\% = 31,5\%$$

SUMMARY OF MANUFACTURING COMPANY LIMITED

The overall assessment of Manufacturing Company Limited is that its performance is healthy with the exceptions possibly of its stock turnover and its average collection period for accounts receivable.

However, throughout the analysis the balance sheet and income statement have been examined for one year only. A more complete evaluation would require at least a 5-year analysis so that trends in sales growth, earnings, dividends and dividend policy can be assessed more fully.

NOTES

NOTES

NOTES

NOTES

NOTES